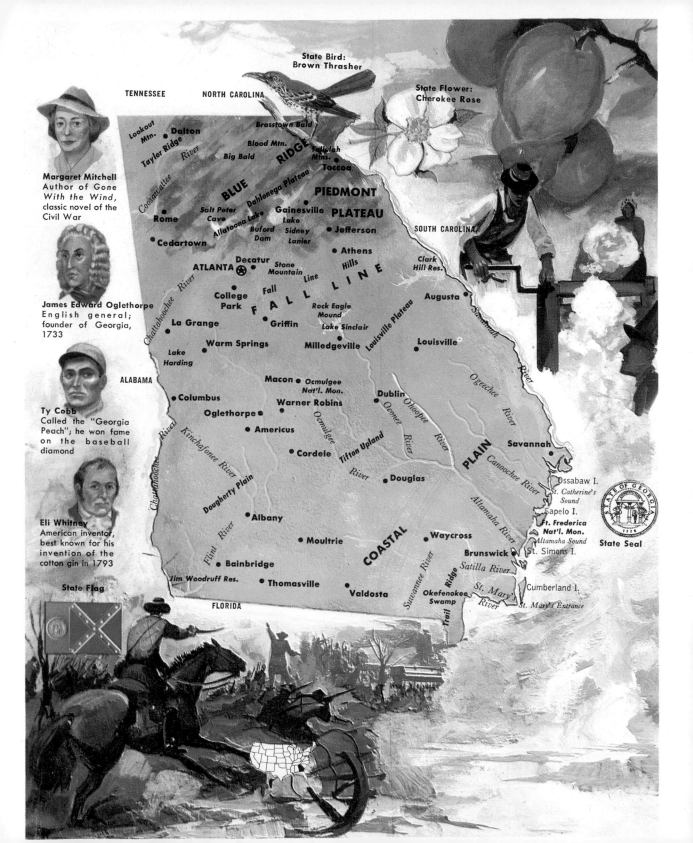

State Bird:
Brown Thrasher

State Flower:
Cherokee Rose

TENNESSEE   NORTH CAROLINA

Margaret Mitchell
Author of *Gone
With the Wind,*
classic novel of the
Civil War

James Edward Oglethorpe
English general;
founder of Georgia,
1733

Ty Cobb
Called the "Georgia
Peach"; he won fame
on the baseball
diamond

Eli Whitney
American inventor,
best known for his
invention of the
cotton gin in 1793

State Flag

Lookout
Mtn.
Taylor Ridge
Dalton
Brasstown Bald
Blood Mtn.
Big Bald
Tallulah
Mtns.
Toccoa
BLUE
RIDGE
Dahlonega Plateau
PIEDMONT
Coosawattee River
Salt Peter
Cave
Allatoona Lake
Gainesville
Lake
PLATEAU
Rome
Buford
Dam
Sidney
Lanier
Jefferson
Cedartown
Athens
SOUTH CAROLINA
ATLANTA
Decatur
Stone
Mountain
Hills
Line
Clark
Hill Res.
Chattahoochee River
College
Park
Fall
FALL LINE
Augusta
La Grange
Griffin
Rock Eagle
Mound
Louisville Plateau
Savannah River
Warm Springs
Lake Sinclair
Milledgeville
Louisville
Lake
Harding
Macon
Ocmulgee
Nat'l. Mon.
Columbus
Warner Robins
Dublin
Oconee River
Oconee River
Ogeechee River
Oglethorpe
Kinchafonee River
Americus
Ohoopee River
PLAIN
Savannah
Chattahoochee River
Cordele
Tifton Upland
River
Ocmulgee River
Canoochee River
Ossabaw I.
St. Catherine's
Sound
Dougherty Plain
Douglas
Sapelo I.
**Ft. Frederica
Nat'l. Mon.**
Altamaha River
Altamaha Sound
St. Simons I.
Albany
Flint River
Moultrie
COASTAL
Waycross
Brunswick
State Seal
STATE OF GEORGIA
Jim Woodruff Res.
Bainbridge
Thomasville
Valdosta
Suwannee River
RIDGE
Satilla River
Cumberland I.
Okefenokee
Swamp
St. Mary's
River
St. Mary's Entrance
Trail
FLORIDA

ALABAMA

GEORGIA: Home of President Jimmy Carter

By Jan Faulk Rogers

 CHILDRENS PRESS, CHICAGO

To a beautiful Georgian, my friend Miss Wessie Connell, Librarian at Roddenbery Memorial Library, Cairo, an inspiration to those who know and love her.

Acknowledgments

Color photography courtesy of the following: Tourist Division, Georgia Department of Industry and Trade, pages 6, 12, 14, 17, 18, 21, 23, 24, 27, 28, 29 (left), 31, 32, 33, 34, 35, 36, 37, 41 and 42; United Press International, Compix, page 10; Stone Mountain Memorial Association, pages 20 and 30; Department of Natural Resources, pages 22, 26, 29 (right), and 38; James Strawser, University of Georgia Cooperative Extension Service, pages 40, 42 (top), and 45 (bottom); Historic Sites Survey, pages 16 and 45 (top).

Cover photograph: President Jimmy Carter, courtesy Lawrence Smith, Chief Photographer, The Ledger-Enquirer Newspapers.

Frontispiece: Covered bridge, courtesy Tourist Division, Georgia Department of Industry and Trade.

Library of Congress Cataloging in Publication Data

Rogers, Jan Faulk.
  Georgia.

  Includes index.
  SUMMARY: A brief description of the history, geography, natural resources, and famous people of Georgia, the largest state east of the Mississippi River.
    1. Georgia—Juvenile literature. 2. Carter, Jimmy, 1924- —Juvenile literature. [1. Georgia]
I. Title
F286.3.R64   975.8   77-20855
ISBN 0-516-03473-1

CONTENTS

The Okefenokee Swamp

INTRODUCTION

Georgia is a land of peaches, pecans, peanuts, pine trees, and presidents. One of the original thirteen colonies, it is the largest state east of the Mississippi River.

From Brasstown Bald Mountain in the beautiful Blue Ridge hills to the mysterious Okefenokee Swamp at the Florida border, history is everywhere.

"George Washington Slept Here" is a claim Georgia can make because President George Washington visited Augusta and Savannah in 1791.

Founded by James Oglethorpe, Georgia has the wonders of Savannah, Eli Whitney's cotton gin, Stone Mountain, Franklin Delano Roosevelt's Little White House, Sherman's March to the Sea, Jekyll Island, Augusta, Atlanta—and now Plains.

TWO FAMOUS GEORGIANS

An unknown peanut farmer, Jimmy Carter, was elected 39th President of the United States in 1976. President Carter is a graduate of the U. S. Naval Academy and was governor of Georgia from 1970 to 1974.

On October 1, 1924, James Earl Carter, Jr., was born in Plains, a small town in Georgia. He took charge of the family farm and warehouse after his father died in 1953. He is also a deacon of the Plains Baptist Church and enjoys teaching Sunday School.

Rosalynn Carter, the President's wife, is called the first lady of the United States. The Carters have three sons, a daughter, and several grandchildren.

Atlanta was the home of Reverend Martin Luther King, Jr., (1929-1968), civil rights leader. He is famous for his speech, "I have a dream." Dr. King worked all his life to make the dream of brotherhood of all men come true. He is responsible for the Civil Rights Act of 1964. Dr. King received the international Nobel Peace Prize.

Dr. King's wife, Coretta, has carried on the work of her husband. She has started the King Center for Social Change in Atlanta.

Above: The Etowah Indian Mounds at Cartersville. Above and bottom left: Artifacts found at the Etowah Indian Mounds.

EARLY HISTORY

Over one thousand years ago, before the white man came, Georgia was the center of religious activity for the Etowah Indians.

The Indians did not move about the land. They built permanent communities and were farmers. They grew corn, pumpkins, beans, and herbs.

The Indians held meetings in huge mounds made of soil. A few mounds, some quite large, are still standing near Cartersville.

The Creeks were another group of Indians. They were living in southern Georgia when the first English settlers came in 1733. James Oglethorpe brought 125 colonists. Chief Tomochichi met the ship at Yamacraw Bluff.

Fort Frederica was built on St. Simons Island in 1736.

Under Oglethorpe's orders, Fort Frederica was built. Georgia served as a buffer between the English colonies and Spanish Florida.

The colony that was named for King George II was very successful.

The colonists started Savannah. Soon settlers from many European countries arrived. They came because they wanted religious freedom.

In 1819 the first steamship, the *SS Savannah,* crossed the Atlantic Ocean from America. When it arrived in England, the people thought it was on fire because of the steam.

Oglethorpe brought John and Charles Wesley to Georgia as missionaries. John is known as the founder of the Methodist Church. He started the first Sunday School in America. The Wesley brothers founded Christ Church on St. Simons Island. Charles returned to England and became a famous preacher and song writer.

Christ Church on
St. Simons Island.

The Cherokee Indians of northern Georgia were very advanced. Chief Sequoyah invented the Cherokee alphabet and taught his people to read and write. Parts of the Bible were translated for the Indians and a newspaper, *The Cherokee Phoenix*, was published. The Indian nation had its own constitution, government, schools, and churches. The Federal government forced the Indians to leave their land. In 1835 the Cherokees moved to reservations west of the Mississippi River.

In 1793 Eli Whitney, while visiting a cotton plantation near Savannah, invented the cotton gin. Gin was short for engine. It separated the cotton seeds from the fibers. The cotton gin helped boost cotton production in the South.

Chief Sequoyah holding his alphabet.

More and more settlers came to Georgia. Wealthy planters from other southern colonies also came, bringing their slaves with them. They laid out large plantations to raise rice, tobacco, and cotton.

Cotton became king in Georgia and was the main crop for many years. Westville, a rebuilt farming village of the 1850s, shows how things were then. Most white settlers owned neither plantations nor slaves. These small farmers were often called rednecks by the plantation owners because they got sunburned working in their fields.

Westville

The Cyclorama, a painting showing the Battle of Atlanta, is at Grant Park in Atlanta.

During the Civil War the Southern states fought the Northern states. In 1861 in Milledgeville, the state capital, Georgia voted to withdraw from the United States. The Southern states formed the Confederate States of America.

Georgia lay in the center of the Confederacy. Atlanta was a leading railroad depot. It was a key city for war supplies.

In 1864 the Northern General William T. Sherman left Chattanooga, Tennessee to conquer Georgia. The battle of Kennesaw Mountain followed. The burning of Atlanta destroyed warehouses, mills, and railroad stations.

Sherman's March to the Sea began. There was a sixty-mile-wide path of destruction through Georgia. Savannah was captured in December. This was General Sherman's Christmas present to President Lincoln.

After the Civil War ended, slavery was illegal. The city of Atlanta and much of Georgia was in ruins.

Stone Mountain is one of the many parks that pays tribute to the Civil War. Three famous Confederate leaders, President Jefferson Davis, General Robert E. Lee, and General Stonewall Jackson are carved on the mountainside.

Many plantations in Thomasville have been restored. On the left is the Greenwood Plantation. Below is the Lapham-Patterson House.

The ante-bellum plantation at the park near Atlanta shows how life was for a few Southerners. Plantation life was shown in the movie *Gone With the Wind.* Margaret Mitchell of Atlanta became famous for writing this novel about the Civil War in Georgia.

Andersonville is the site of the largest prison camp used by the Confederacy during the Civil War. Tombstones remind visitors of those who have died in wars.

In 1868, mainly because of its
location, Atlanta became the capital of
Georgia. Atlanta grew rapidly into a
national city. It is known for education,
industry, transportation, government,
and entertainment. Coca-Cola was first
sold in a drug store in Atlanta.

Restored row houses in Savannah

SPECIAL PLACES

Georgia is the largest state east of the Mississippi River. More than half of the state is in the flat Coastal Plain.

The land gets higher toward the north. The hilly region forms the Piedmont Plateau.

The northern section of Georgia is in the mountains.

In the southeastern part of the state is the Okefenokee Swamp, where wild ducks, bears, opossums, wildcats, and alligators live. The Seminole Indians called the swamp "land of the trembling earth," because the earth shook. Its 700-square-mile area of

Cumberland Island's unspoiled seashore.

wilderness gives rise to the Suwanee
River. The wildlife sanctuary protects
its creatures from guns, traps, and the
advance of civilization.

Off the Georgia coast lies a chain of
islands. The most important are Jekyll,
St. Simons, Tybee, Cumberland,
Ossabaw, St. Catherine's, and Amelia.

Georgia's Golden Isles were once the playground of the wealthy. Today the area is a family vacation spot open to all. Located on the ocean, the islands offer year round fishing and swimming. The hundred miles of Atlantic shoreline are famous for their unspoiled beauty.

Sidney Lanier, born in Macon, has been called the South's finest poet. "The Marshes of Glynn" was his most important poem. The wide sea marshes of Glynn are the largest salt marshes on the East Coast.

The Marshes of Glynn

Callaway Gardens is a famous 2,500
acre family resort. It features wild
flowers of the southern Appalachian
Mountains. The seasonal display in the
gardens is well known. Year round
sports and activities attract visitors.

The Rock Eagle 4-H Center has a huge rock formation made from milky quartz. The Indian-made memorial measures 102 feet from head to tail and 120 feet from wing tip to wing tip.

Dahlonega, the mountain community, was the site of the first gold rush in American history, in 1830. Panning for gold at the Gold Hills of Dahlonega is as exciting as it was during the first major gold rush. The dome of the state capitol building is covered with native gold.

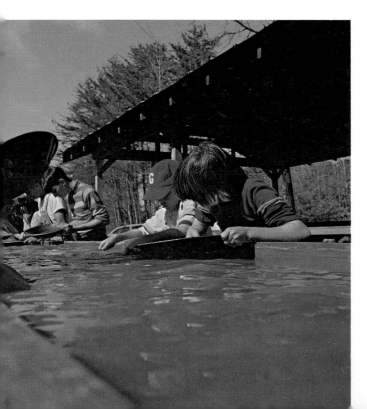

Left: Panning for gold. Below: The dome on the capitol building.

Today many families visit Stone Mountain Park. They can take a paddleboat ride on the lake or a train ride around the mountain.

Helen, a small Alpine village, was created in the natural beauty of the mountains.

Georgia can be fun at all times. Few states offer such a variety of weather and natural beauty.

In the mountains, camping, hiking, fishing, and snow skiing are popular.

Golf is king at the famous Masters' Golf Tournament in Augusta and at the Atlanta Classic.

Atlanta International Raceway has annual stock car races.

Fishing, skiing, and
stock car racing are
popular in Georgia.

Professional baseball, football,
hockey, and basketball add to the
excitement of Atlanta.

Hank Aaron at bat.

Jackie Robinson, from Cairo
was the first black in major leagu
baseball.
Hank Aaron overtook Babe
Ruth's record when he hit hi
715th home run in Atlanta in 1974
Ty Cobb, in the Baseball Hall o
Fame, and Bobby Jones, one of the
greatest golfers of all times, wer
born in Augusta.

The Atlanta Flames.

Above: An unfinished portrait of President Roosevelt is in the Little White House (left).

Franklin Delano Roosevelt was President of the United States for four times. He was crippled by polio. He came to Warm Springs to swim in the warm waters. He loved the Little White House where he died on April 12.

Festivals and fairs, such as Dogwood, Apple, Watermelon, and Sweet Potato festivals, honor some of the state's products. Rattlesnake roundup and the Mule Day Celebration are special events.

Eatonton is proud of its native son, Joel Chandler Harris, and his famous Uncle Remus stories. He wrote about Brer (Brother) Rabbit and Brer Fox.

Beautiful flowers are found
in all areas of Georgia.

Thomasville is famous for its Rose
Parade and Show. The City of Roses
has daily tours of beautiful plantations
and gardens.

Shrimp boats in the harbor at Brunswick.

NATURAL RESOURCES

Georgia has many rivers. The Chattahoochee and Flint rivers flow into the Gulf of Mexico. The Savannah River flows into the Atlantic Ocean. It forms most of the state border between South Carolina and Georgia. Columbus and Augusta are port cities of the rivers.

Brunswick is a busy seaport. Fresh seafood is available along the Georgia coast. The shrimp boats provide income for many fishermen.

Georgia is nearly as large as New England. The state is 320 miles long from Florida on the south to Tennessee and North Carolina on the north. It is 260 miles wide from Alabama on the west to South Carolina on the east.

Cotton is one of
Georgia's leading
farm products.

Cotton textile production is a major part of Georgia's economy. Along with carpet mills, the cotton mills make the state the major textile producer in the nation. Clothes, towels, and sheets are manufactured.

Airplanes, automobiles, mobile homes, paper bags, and chemicals are a few of the other products made in Georgia.

The pine forests of Georgia yield pulpwood for paper, plastics, and turpentine. Fine wood for furniture and flooring comes from the mountain forests. Wooden boxes and barrels are made from soft woods.

Pine forests in the north.

Right: Tobacco buyers examine the crop. Below: The old mill wheel, a symbol of Berry College.

Marble from Georgia's quarries was used in the beautiful Lincoln Memorial in Washington, D. C.

The warm climate, good soil, and long growing season in Georgia help agriculture.

Southern Georgia is known for its tobacco. Many acres are grown under shade, or tents, to protect the large leaves.

Georgia leads the nation in the production of chickens. It also markets hogs, beef, eggs, milk, and turkeys.

Martha Berry read Bible stories to mountain children. She taught them how to read, write, and think. She started the famous Berry Schools in Rome, Georgia, in 1902. The students worked to pay for their tuition.

Rebecca L. Felton of Georgia became the first woman U.S. senator in 1922.

Georgia is the leader in the production of pecans and peanuts. Peaches, watermelons, apples, and blueberries are grown. Sweet potatoes, tomatoes, okra, cucumbers, beans, and corn are a few of the vegetables sold at the Atlanta Farmers' Market, the world's largest.

There are many important Georgians. Crawford W. Long, from Danielsville, was the first doctor to use ether as an anesthetic in surgery. Julian Bond, a civil rights leader, was the first black Congressman since Reconstruction. Andrew Young became America's Ambassador to the United Nations in 1977.

Because of its size and industries, Georgia is called the *Empire State of the South.*

Savannah was the birthplace of Juliette Gordon Low, founder of the Girl Scouts of the United States. The first Girl Scout troop was started in 1912 with her niece, Daisy Gordon, as the first member. The Girl Scouts have made the Low home into a scouting shrine.

Left: The Juliette Gordon Low home. Below: Part of Farmers' Market in Atlanta.

IMPORTANT DATES

1733—Oglethorpe settles in Georgia with 125 colonists
1788—Georgia becomes a state, January 2
1793—Whitney invents the cotton gin
1819—*SS Savannah* crosses the Atlantic Ocean
1830—First gold rush in America, at Dahlonega
1835—Cherokee Indians move to reservations west of the Mississippi River
1842—Anesthetic first used during surgery
1861—Civil War begins
1961—Georgia votes to withdraw from the United States, January 19
1864—Sherman conquers Georgia, burns Atlanta
1865—Civil War ends
1868—Atlanta becomes capital of Georgia
1891—George Washington visits Augusta and Savannah
1902—Berry Schools begin in Rome, Georgia
1912—First Girl Scout troop in America, started by Juliette Gordon Low
1922—Rebecca L. Felton becomes the first woman U. S. Senator
1924—James Earl Carter, Jr. born, October 1
1929—Martin Luther King, Jr. born, January 15
1945—Franklin Delano Roosevelt dies at Warm Springs, April 12
1964—Civil Rights Act passed, April 4
1964—Reverend Martin Luther King, Jr. receives Nobel Peace Prize
1968—Reverend Martin Luther King, Jr. assassinated, April 4
1970—Jimmy Carter becomes governor of Georgia
1974—Hank Aaron breaks Babe Ruth's home-run record
1976—Jimmy Carter elected 39th President
1977—Andrew Young becomes U. S. Ambassador to the United Nations

INDEX

ABOUT THE AUTHOR

Jan Faulk Rogers received her B. A. and M. S. degrees in library science from Florida State University. While attending the university, she became a member of Beta Phi Mu, Library Science Honorary, and American Library Association. In addition to her studies, she was a library employee in Cairo, Georgia, specializing in childrens' work. As children's librarian, Jan frequently had speaking engagements at teachers' clinics, library organizations, and summer programs. Children and their reading needs became apparent to her through her close contact with them.

While working with young children in libraries and in the Georgia school system, Jan discovered a need for more history-oriented material. She has developed her pet project of state history into this book, and has also written *First Lady: Rosalynn Carter.*

Jan is now School Library Co-ordinator in Spalding County, Griffin, Georgia, where she continues working for children's needs.

Jan and her husband, Robert, and their two daughters, Jana and Rebecca spend their leisure time on their farm and restored country home south of Atlanta. They enjoy gardening, handicrafts, and growing their own vegetables and fruits.